Oceans of Resources

by J. F. Culbertson

PEARSON
Scott Foresman

Editorial Offices: Glenview, Illinois • Parsippany, New Jersey • New York, New York
Sales Offices: Needham, Massachusetts • Duluth, Georgia • Glenview, Illinois
Coppell, Texas • Ontario, California • Mesa, Arizona

Every effort has been made to secure permission and provide appropriate credit for photographic material. The publisher deeply regrets any omission and pledges to correct errors called to its attention in subsequent editions.

Unless otherwise acknowledged, all photographs are the property of Scott Foresman, a division of Pearson Education.

Photo locators denoted as follows: Top (T), Center (C), Bottom (B), Left (L), Right (R), Background (Bkgd)

Opener ©George H. H. Huey/Corbis; 1 ©Vincent Leloup/Corbis; 3 ©Royalty-Free/Corbis; 4 © Natalie Fobes/Corbis; 6 ©Annie Griffiths Belt/Corbis; 7 ©Natalie Fobes/Corbis; 9 ©Natalie Fobes/Corbis; 13 ©R. Toms/OSF/Animals Animals/Earth Scenes; 14 ©Vincent Leloup/Corbis; 15 ©S.Lowry/Univ Ulster/Stone/Getty Images; 17 ©Royalty-Free/Corbis; 18 ©Michael S. Yamashita/Corbis; 19 ©Daniel Joubert/Reuters/Corbis; 20 ©Dallas and John Heaton/Free Agents Limited/Corbis; 21 ©George H. H. Huey/Corbis; 22 ©Gustavo Gilabert/Corbis; 23 ©Arthur Tilley/Getty Images

ISBN: 0-328-13579-8

8 9 10 V0G1 14 13 12 11 10 09 08

A Watery World

Earth is a blue, water-covered planet. More than seventy percent of Earth's surface is ocean. That's almost 145 million square miles of water, making Earth the wettest planet in the solar system. While Earth's human inhabitants live on land, they rely on the oceans to provide many of their needs. Food, transportation, minerals, recreation, and even energy are all important ocean resources for humans around the globe.

A large commercial fishing vessel, operating miles from shore, is capable of bringing back a haul of fish weighing in at tens of thousands of pounds.

The Ocean's Bounty

Humans have relied on the oceans for food since the dawn of prehistory. Huge mounds of oyster, clam, and snail shells help anthropologists—scientists who study how humans lived—identify the locations where the earliest settlements occurred.

Mollusks, such as oysters, clams, and snails, could simply be gathered along the shore. Fish had to be caught, and early humans developed traps and nets for doing this. As technology improved—the development of boats, the development of hooks—fishing became more effective.

As fishing techniques improved, dependency on fish increased. Fishing boats went out farther and farther in search of large schools of the tastiest fish. It seemed that the ocean's bounty was inexhaustible.

In fact, humans have always captured only a small portion of the ocean's fish. Whales, seals, and other marine life consume vastly more sea life than humans do. But over time, fishing techniques became so efficient that what we were taking out of the water was simply too much, and the balance changed. While there are still many fish in the ocean, some of the richest fishing grounds are now nearly empty.

Crabs are among the many foods people get from the oceans.

Aquaculture: Fish Farming

Because of this lack of fish, many popular fish have become expensive or have disappeared from the marketplace. Most countries today respect fishing treaties that are designed to help rebuild traditional fishing grounds. It is hoped that, if fishing is stopped for a while or strictly limited, fish will have a chance to multiply once again.

But while wild fish populations have shrunk, the demand for fish is growing. Fish is high in both protein and certain compounds that nutritionists believe may contribute to having a healthy heart. People are eating more fish as part of a healthier diet. In the past twenty-five years, world consumption of fish has doubled. While much fish is still caught in the wild, people around the world depend increasingly on fish farming, or aquaculture.

The Chinese have been fish farming for about four thousand years. Chinese aquaculture produces seaweeds as well as carp. In Japan, many varieties of fish and **shellfish** are raised, as well as seaweeds. Europe adds eels to their aquaculture list. Russia favors sturgeon, for its famous caviar. North American fish farmers raise trout, catfish, salmon, shrimp, and oysters.

Most ocean aquaculture is done close to the coast or in large tanks. But some people are trying to farm fish farther from shore. In one such experiment off the Atlantic coast, net pens, specially designed to contain fish in the open ocean, have been placed 180 feet below the surface.

Much of the salmon eaten in the United States today was raised on fish farms, not caught in the wild.

Many fish farms are close to shore. This has created some problems, and it has some oceanographers and marine biologists worried about aquaculture's effect on ocean **ecosystems**. These fish farms can pollute coastal waters that would not normally have so many fish nearby. Some people also worry that fish raised in unnatural habitats will not be as wholesome for those who rely on the fish as food.

The National Oceanic and Atmospheric Administration (NOAA), an agency of the United States Department of Commerce, wants to see aquaculture developed further. The agency is encouraging companies to develop ways to farm fish offshore that are safe for the ocean ecosystems, and the agency offers funding for such projects. One company sank a twelve-sided fish pen thirty-five feet beneath the ocean's surface, two miles off the coast of Puerto Rico. The pen is filled with two kinds of fish: snapper and cobia. Cables connect the pens to small marker buoys floating on the surface.

These fish pens don't pollute the coastline as do those closer to shore. In the open ocean, hundreds of gallons of water pass through the pen, washing away leftover food and waste.

Raising fish offshore in deep underwater pens will likely become more common in the future.

More Bounty from the Sea

Fish and other seafood for the table aren't the only things being harvested from the ocean. Seaweed, which is rich in the essential mineral iodine, is another important ocean food for many Asians, as well as for a growing number of Americans.

Fishmeal is another ocean product. It's made of ground-up, dried fish. Fishmeal is added to animal feed and can also be processed into the human food called fish protein concentrate (FPC). FPC has no taste or odor and provides a protein boost to soups and other foods. It may someday help feed starving people.

Scientists are also searching the ocean for new medicines. Researchers have discovered that a chemical from a small animal called a sea squirt may shrink **tumors**. And a chemical found in sponges may help cure certain skin diseases, while other ocean substances being looked at may kill germs or lower blood pressure.

Salt and Water

People have long harvested sea salt by allowing the sun to evaporate seawater and then collecting the salt left behind. Salt can also be removed from seawater to create another precious resource—fresh water. This process is called desalination. There are many desalination facilities that turn seawater into freshwater. Saudi Arabia has the largest, producing about 600 million gallons of freshwater a day.

There are several desalination methods used today. Some force seawater through filters that take out the salt. Others **distill** the water, heating it until it evaporates and then collecting the pure water that condenses. Solar distillation is a very old practice. Julius Caesar's soldiers made drinking water with solar stills more than two thousand years ago.

The Solar Still

In a solar still, seawater is placed in a dark-colored shallow container and topped with a clear, sloping cover. The dark color helps the sun heat up the seawater and cause it to evaporate. The water vapor condenses on the cover and trickles down into a collection trough. The salt is left behind in the container.

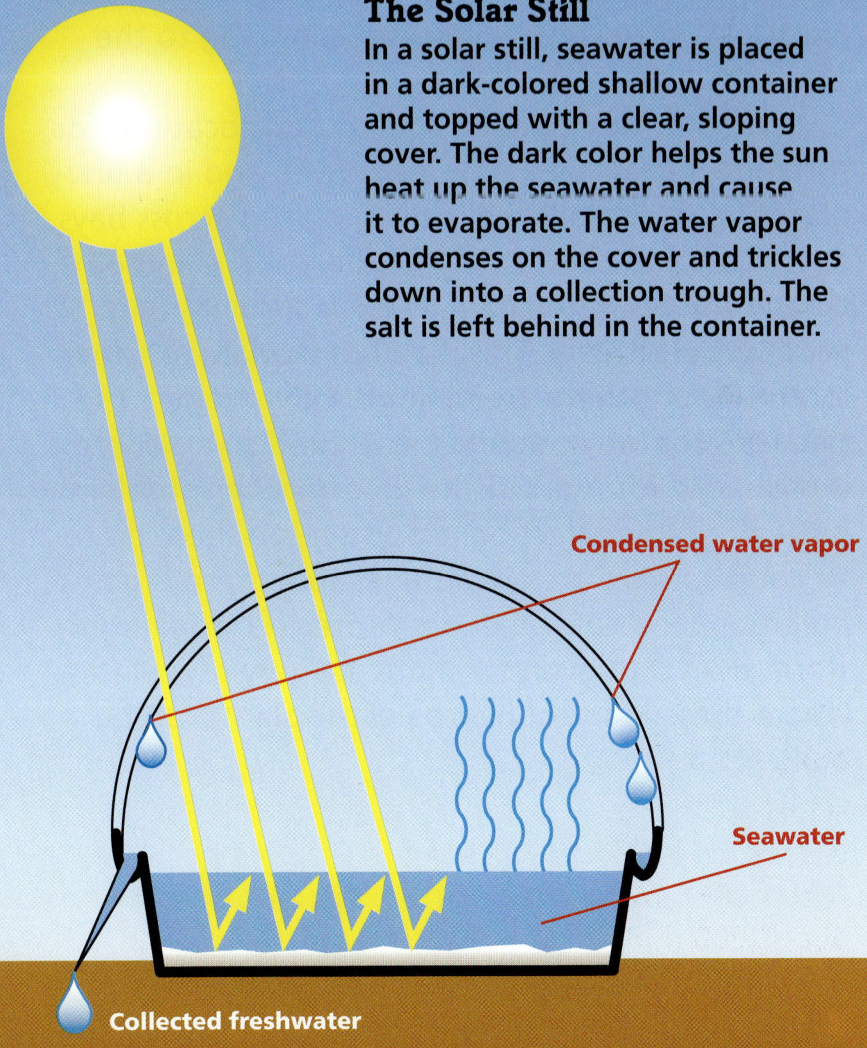

An Ocean of Power

Throughout history, humans have put the power of moving water to work. They have relied on tides and currents for transportation and streams for turning waterwheels to grind grain or run saws. Since the 1800s, running or falling water has been used to generate electricity. **Hydroelectric** plants house huge **turbines**, which are turned by the rushing water, transforming the water's energy into electricity. As demands for new, cleaner sources of electricity increase, engineers are looking to the ocean.

One solution has been to find new locations for turbines. Tides have immense power, and in a few places, massive dams have been placed across bays to capture this power. As the tide goes in and out through gates in the dam, it turns turbines and produces electricity. This plan has worked in a few locations, but there are major disadvantages. The tide runs for only ten hours each day, so no energy is produced for most of the day. Another problem is the dramatic effect on ecosystems in these bays. Of course, there are advantages too; there is no pollution, and coastlines are protected from high storm tides. But even so, there are very few places where these kinds of hydroelectric plants can be built.

This tidal power station in France was built in 1966. It is the largest tidal power station in the world.

Some people think that the answer is to put turbines offshore because ocean currents are very reliable. Because no dams are needed, coastal ecosystems are not damaged. Experiments with these offshore turbines began in 2003, and so far, they look promising. Studies seem to indicate that this technology would not pose a danger to fish or marine mammals.

Another experimental technology is ocean thermal energy conversion, or OTEC. Every day, the oceans soak up an amount of **solar** energy equivalent to the energy produced by burning 250 billion barrels of oil. OTEC aims to turn this energy into electricity. Successful tests have been run, which has given hope to places with abundant ocean resources, such as the Hawaiian Islands.

Europe already has a number of offshore wind farms.

Energy may be found above the waves, as well as beneath them. Windmills have been harvesting the power of wind for centuries. Modern wind farms generate a great deal of electricity today. Success on land has increased interest in putting wind farms on the ocean too. The ocean is a logical place for a wind farm. From trade winds to tropical storms, winds blow across the oceans almost constantly, with nothing to slow them down. Unlike power plants that burn fossil fuels, wind farms don't produce the polluting gases that may contribute to global warming.

Not everyone agrees that offshore wind farms are a good idea, though. Some environmental and wildlife protection groups argue that the turbines might harm migrating birds. Others worry that they could also harm the fishing industry. Some people don't like the windmills simply because they ruin the ocean view.

The debate is likely to continue for some time. Not everyone agrees on how these technologies affect the ocean, and not everyone has the same goals or priorities. While the ocean holds great promise as a renewable source of energy, the technical and economic challenges are great. Protecting ocean ecosystems while harvesting energy is perhaps the greatest challenge of all.

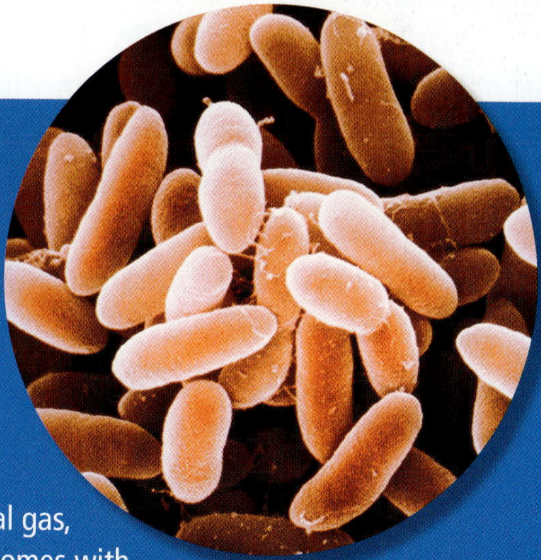

Gas from Sea Microbes

In 1983 an unusual life form was discovered in the Pacific Ocean. It's a microbe that can grow in complete darkness called *Methanococcus jannaschii.* The microbe also produces methane. Methane is natural gas, the gas we cook and heat homes with. Researchers are now investigating how to make the microbe produce more methane. Perhaps someday you'll cook with gas from an ocean microbe!

Ocean Fertilization: A Solution to Global Warming?

From a New Yorker running his car to a farmer in Argentina burning his fields before planting, much of what we do creates carbon dioxide. When you breathe out, you are releasing carbon dioxide into the **atmosphere**. Carbon dioxide, along with other atmospheric gases, creates a protective barrier that lets the warmth of the sun in but does not let it all escape—much as a greenhouse works. Without this barrier, the planet would be frozen and lifeless. However, in recent years, because of the growing number of cars and factories worldwide, carbon dioxide has increased rapidly. Some scientists believe that an excess of carbon dioxide may keep in too much heat, causing global warming.

Some scientists are looking to the oceans for ways to remove excess carbon dioxide from our atmosphere. One idea is ocean fertilization. We would put fertilizer in the ocean to increase the number of small ocean life forms called phytoplankton. Phytoplankton convert sunlight and carbon dioxide into food through photosynthesis, like plants do. More phytoplankton in the ocean would take more carbon dioxide from the atmosphere. However, no one knows how increasing phytoplankton would affect the ocean's ecosystems. Ocean fertilization might create more problems than it solves.

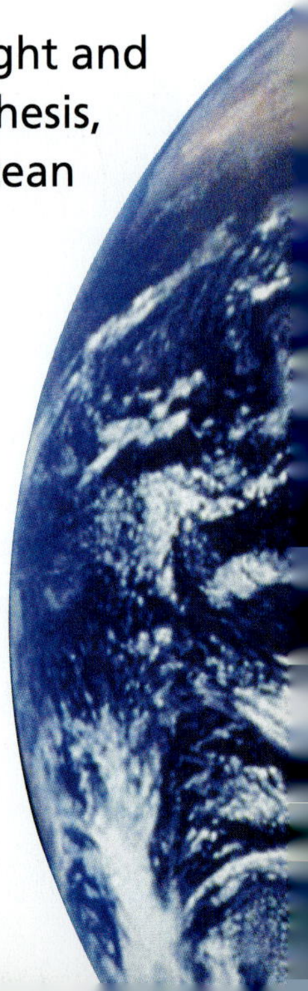

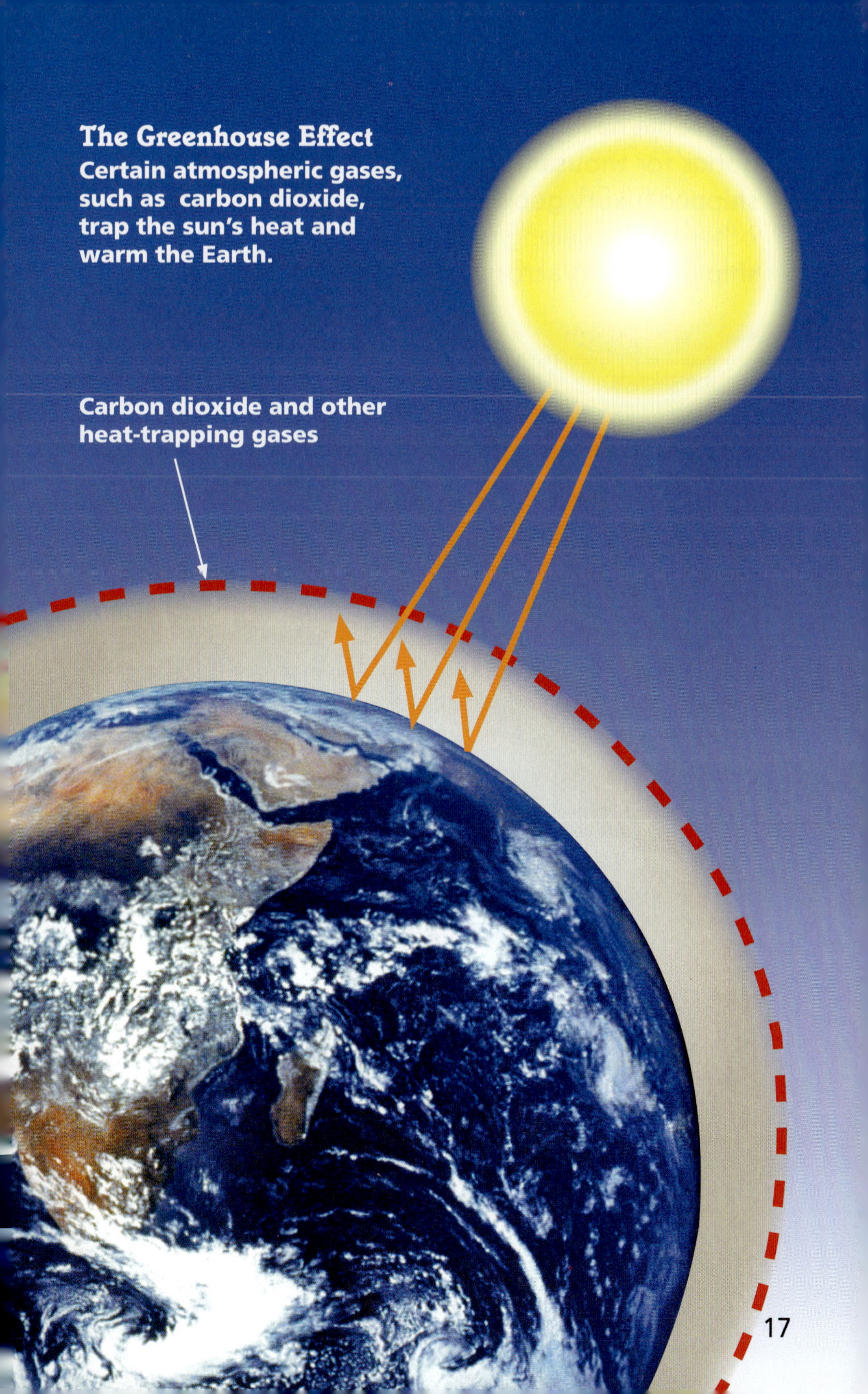

The Greenhouse Effect
Certain atmospheric gases, such as carbon dioxide, trap the sun's heat and warm the Earth.

Our Watery Highway

People have used the seas to travel and transport goods for thousands of years. Ancient civilizations shipped luxury goods like spices, as well as grain and other staples, along sea passages. We continue to ship our goods across the world's oceans today.

Modern ocean-going cargo ships transport everything from oil and grain to toys and books.

Supertankers carry oil. Container ships carry boxes of goods so large that cranes must load them. Cars are shipped over the ocean's waves. Even some of the rockets we send into space travel to the launch pad by ship.

Ships once carried every passenger who traveled over an ocean. Today most people take airplanes when traveling overseas. But some travelers still choose to board ocean liners to experience a more leisurely trip or get a taste of times past.

The Queen Mary 2 is the most expensive and largest luxury ocean liner ever built.

Traveling in Style

Flying from New York to London takes about six hours. That same voyage on the *Queen Mary 2 (QM2)* takes six days. During those six days you can play golf or basketball, attend the theater, dine at fancy restaurants, and even shop! The *QM2* is a huge luxury ocean liner. Passengers can stroll along a deck that encircles the ship in a loop one-third of a mile long. If the clouds hide the stars at night, passengers can even enjoy their stargazing in the ship's planetarium.

People all over the world love to spend time at the beach.

What's your favorite ocean scene?

A Day at the Beach

Another resource from the world's oceans is recreation. Spending time at the beach sunning, swimming, or searching for shells is many people's idea of the perfect vacation! Surfing, sailing, ocean swimming, and deep-sea fishing are popular pastimes all over the world. The ocean is a source of recreation and tourism money for many coastal and island communities.

If you're lucky enough to live near the sea, you may take it for granted. If you've never been to the ocean, it may be something only seen on television or in the movies. Watching sunlight sparkle on the vast water and listening to waves breaking on rocks have inspired poets and painters for generations. It might inspire you, as well, someday. The world's oceans themselves are a precious resource.

Now Try This

How can pollution like this be prevented?

As you've just read, the world's oceans are a natural resource that provide food, energy, transportation, recreation, inspiration, and more. Like all of our natural resources, the oceans are threatened by misuse and pollution. Oil tanker spills cause environmental disasters. Factories and ships dumping pollutants into the sea foul the water and harm ocean ecosystems. Trash dumped thousands of miles away washes up on beaches around the world.

What can you do to help keep the oceans healthy? Put together a clean-up-the-beach campaign for a shoreline near you. (If you don't live near the ocean, put together a campaign for a local lake or river.)

Here's How to Do It!

1. First, make a list of some ways our waters become polluted. You might want to do a little research in the library or on the Internet to complete your list.
2. Next, think of the reasons that people should care about keeping our waters free of pollution. What do people lose when waters become polluted?
3. Write a slogan for your campaign to end pollution of our waters. Remember that a slogan needs to be short, to the point, and easy for people to understand and remember.
4. Design a poster for your campaign. Illustrate the poster with your own drawings or with photographs of local pollution problems. Remind people of the kind of pollution that exists by including some of the items from step 1 above. Also remind people why they should want to fight pollution by including items from step 2. Print your slogan on poster board so that it's easy to read. Perhaps your teacher will want you to display your poster in the classroom.

Trash harms ocean wildlife.

Glossary

atmosphere *n.* the air surrounding Earth.

distill *v.* to heat a liquid until it evaporates in order to purify it.

ecosystems *n.* physical environments and the communities of plants and animals that inhabit them.

hydroelectric *adj.* producing electricity by using the power of moving water.

shellfish *n.* soft-bodied ocean animals with shells or shell-like coverings, such as clams, oysters, shrimp, and lobsters.

solar *adj.* of or from the sun.

tumors *n.* abnormal growths.

turbines *n.* spinning engines that create electricity.